BewareofArtists.org

One Liners

Volume 1

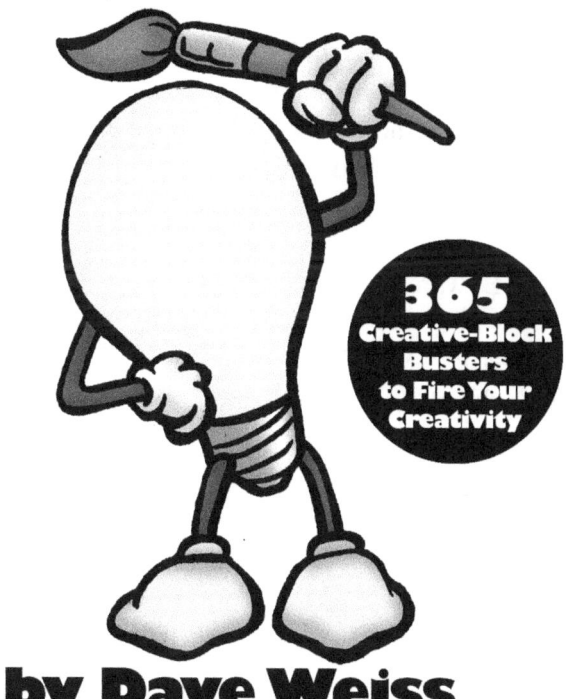

365 Creative-Block Busters to Fire Your Creativity

by Dave Weiss

A Beware of Artists Creativity Resource

www.BewareofArtists.org

ISBN-10: 1481033174
ISBN-13: 978-1481033176

Manufactured in the United States of America

What is a One-Liner?

Did you ever have one of those days when you really wanted to create something, but the ideas just weren't flowing? That is the purpose of a One-Liner. It might be a phrase, a sentence or even just a word, but it's enough to get your creativity moving.

These "creative-block busters" are designed to get you thinking, make pictures in your mind and start you into the creative process. Draw a picture. Sketch in your journal. Write a story or a poem. Take some photos. From there, the sky's the limit.

How to use this book...

The short answer is use it how you want. It's organized by day, 365 One-Liners, one for each day of the year, but you certainly don't have to use it that way. If today's prompt doesn't fire your imagination, look for one that does. Order is not important, as a matter of fact order can be just another creative-block. What IS important is that you start creating. You might read a One-Liner and it might take you in a whole different direction—that's okay, run with it and create.

All I want to do with this book is get you creating. If you start creating, it has done it's work. So... what are you waiting for? Jump in and start creating!

Have Fun!

January 1
What does the Baby New Year face in the year ahead?

_____

January 2
It's now politically correct to call the holiday parties "winter celebration." What is there to celebrate about winter?

_____

January 3
It's J.R.R. Tolkien's birthday. Draw your favorite resident of Middle Earth.

January 4

Where would you rather be right now?

_____

January 5

The world's greatest snowman

_____

January 6

What is a bleacher creature?

January 7
My fondest snow day memory is…

_____

January 8
The worst thing about winter weather is…

_____

January 9
The best thing about winter weather is…

January 10
Two Words: Cabin Fever!

_____

January 11
Snowball battle

_____

January 12
What is your family pet thinking right now?

January 13
Worst Billboard Ever

_____

January 14
The best decision I have ever made is…

_____

January 15
The best book I've ever read is…

January 16

It's Martin Luther King Day. How should we honor Dr. King?

January 17

It's Benjamin Franklin's birthday. Draw your favorite Franklin invention or invent something of your own.

January 18

Time flies when you're having fun. What does time do when you're not?

January 19

Color outside the lines. Let's show those lines who's boss.

_____

January 20

It's Inauguration Day in the U.S. What should the president accomplish this term?

_____

January 21

Creative people must create.

January 22
Two months to Spring! How does that make you feel?

January 23
It's Chinese New Year, 2013, the year of the snake!

January 24
All that glitters is not gold but then again, all that glitters isn't glitter.

January 25
How do they know no two snowflakes are alike?

_____

January 26
Is politically correct an oxymoron?

_____

January 27
What is the one thing you simply can't do without?

January 28

Everyone leaves a legacy. What's yours?

_____

January 29

Sketch a copy of your favorite work of art.

_____

January 30

It's FDR's birthday. He once said "We have nothing to fear but fear itself…" and then I added , Well… that and
_____.

January 31
Why don't humans hibernate?

_____

February 1
It's National Freedom Day in the U.S. What does freedom mean to you?

_____

February 2
It's Groundhog Day. If it was up to you, what would the groundhog see? Or How much wood would a woodchuck chuck if a woodchuck could chuck wood?

February 3

What was the highlight of the Superbowl for you?

_____

February 4

Draw a portrait of your favorite artist.

_____

February 5

Redesign the logo of your favorite soft drink.

February 6
What's your favorite winter activity?

_____

February 7
Draw a furry whats-it.

_____

February 8
Beware of artists…

February 9
Be humble or be humbled.

_____

February 10
Happy is the man who...

_____

February 11
Happy is the woman who...

February 12

It's Abraham Lincoln's Birthday, draw a picture of this great president.

―――――――――――――――

February 13

Tomorrow is Valentine's Day. Make a card for someone special.

―――――――――――――――

February 14

Worst Valentine Card Ever

February 15

It's The Simpsons creator Matt Groening's Birthday, draw yourself as a character on the show.

_____

February 16

Worst Superhero Ever

_____

February 17

What is the title of your biography? Draw the cover.

February 18

One thing everyone should know is...

_____

February 19

Take your passion and make it happen.

_____

February 20

It's Love Your Pet Day.

February 21
It's President's Day in the US. Draw your favorite leader.

_____

February 22
It's George Washington's Birthday. Draw a picture of the father of our country.

_____

February 23
A dream is just reality waiting for its time.

February 24

_____ is the root of all evil.

_____

February 25

The secret to my success is...

_____

February 26

_____ is a virtue.

February 27

The thing of which I am most proud is...

_____

February 28

The most important thing I have every done is...

_____

March 1

March is National Craft Month. Do something crafty.

March 2

It's Dr. Seuss' birthday. Draw your favorite of his characters.

———————————————

March 3

Draw a portrait of your childhood hero.

———————————————

March 4

March comes in like a lion…

March 5

What makes you truly happy?

_____

March 6

Cause and effect

_____

March 7

Design a better mousetrap.

March 8
Draw a crying onion.

_____

March 9
Define Art.

_____

March 10
My imaginary friend thinks I have mental problems.

March 11
Design your dream car.

_____

March 12
The sign I'd like to hang over my desk says...

_____

March 13
Worst Sporting Event Ever

March 14

A vision is reality waiting for you to create it.

―――――――――――――

March 15

Let your imagination run wild.

―――――――――――――

March 16

I'm going crazy! Anyone care to join me?

March 17
Liam the Leprechaun traded his pot of gold for a pot of

_____

_____

March 18
The greatest invention in human history is...

_____

March 19
I'm only human...

March 20

The early bird gets…

_____

March 21

Spring puts a Spring in my step.

_____

March 22

Draw your favorite sign of spring.

March 23

The best person I know is...

_____

March 24

Preparing for the panda apocalypse...

_____

March 25

It's not that easy being...

March 26
My favorite place in the world is...

_____

March 27
Worst game show ever

_____

March 28
And the award for best _____ goes to...

March 29

March goes out like a lamb.

_____

March 30

It's Vincent Van Gogh's Birthday. Sketch your favorite
of his paintings or do one of your own in his style.

_____

March 31

Today the Christian world celebrates Easter. What is
your favorite expression of the day?

April 1
It's April Fool's Day! Have at it!

———————————————

April 2
It's National Humor Month. Draw something funny.

———————————————

April 3
Living on a dessert island (Yes, I spelled it that way on purpose!)

April 4
Draw something silly.

_____

April 5
If teddy bears ruled the world...

_____

April 6
Design your personal logo.

April 7

The solution to my greatest problem is...

_____

April 8

The one thing we really need is...

_____

April 9

Who am I and why am I here?

April 10
The greatest invention ever...

April 11
Our culture is getting so health conscious, I just saw a margarine fly.

April 12
Karate Koala

April 13
Worst April Fool's Joke Ever

_____

April 14
If I wanted drama, I'd go to the theater.

_____

April 15
In the U.S. it's tax day. How does that make you feel?

April 16

Everything I ever really needed to know, I learned in…

_____

April 17

_____ always makes me smile.

_____

April 18

Create a meme that tells the world how you feel.

April 19

Charles Darwin passed away on this date in 1882. In honor of his life's work, why are there still monkeys?

_____

April 20

They're carving a new Mt. Rushmore. Whose faces should be on it?

_____

April 21

My favorite childhood cartoon character

April 22

Go fly a kite!

April 23

If you will want my help with the consequences of your actions, please see me before you do them.

April 24

Why do they call sick people patients?

April 25
Archeologists have discovered a new dinosaur.

_____

April 26
Easter has the bunny, Christmas has Santa, who is the person for Arbor Day?

_____

April 27
I'm happier than a....

April 28
What's your favorite part of the day?

_____

April 29
Combat Wombat

_____

April 30
Draw what you feel right now.

May 1
MAY DAY! MAY DAY!

_____

May 2
The most beautiful thing I've ever seen is…

_____

May 3
How many artists does it take to change a light bulb?

May 4
It's Keith Haring's birthday. Do a piece of art in his style.

_____

May 5
When _____s fly…

_____

May 6
The argument you know you can't win…

May 7

The most obnoxious thing in the world is…

_____

May 8

Draw the flowers the April showers brought.

_____

May 9

Go against the flow.

May 10
Passive Aggressive Possum

_____

May 11
Tomorrow is Mother's Day. Make mom a card or present!

_____

May 12
Design a T-shirt for your all-time favorite band.

May 13
Worst Invention Ever

May 14
It's George Lucas' Birthday. Draw your favorite Star Wars Character.

May 15
It's L. Frank Baum's Birthday. Draw your favorite denizen of the land of Oz.

May 16
Dinosaur Picnic

_____

May 17
What's a schnugiflargen?

_____

May 18
Kung fu Kangaroo

May 19
What do you want to do this summer?

_____

May 20
Draw a used car salesman.

_____

May 21
To fail to plan is to plan to fail.

May 22

Thomas Edison failed a thousand times before creating a working light bulb. When asked how it felt to fail so many times, he said, "I didn't fail, I learned a thousand ways not to make a light bulb." What can you learn from your mistakes?

_____

May 23

Smart people learn from other people's mistakes.

_____

May 24

What motivates you?

May 25
Draw a brainstorm.

––––––––––––––––––––

May 26
Create a tropical fish.

––––––––––––––––––––

May 27
It's Memorial Day. Make something to show you remember.

May 28
Who deserves the next monument?

_____

May 29
What I'm going to do on my summer vacation...

_____

May 30
If I had a million dollars, Id'...

May 31
What are you reading this summer? Redesign the cover.

June 1
No matter where he goes, the turtle is always at home.

June 2
It takes a few clouds to make a beautiful sunrise.

June 3
Gorilla Milkshake

_____

June 4
Dinosaur Picnic

_____

June 5
June is listed as Fight the Filthy Fly Month. How will you do your part?

June 6
This summer's biggest blockbuster.

_____

June 7
Hurry up and wait!

_____

June 8
Warhol, the fifth karate tortoise (or something like that).

June 9

Draw a decorative sun or other summer symbol.

_____

June 10

Life's a beach!

_____

June 11

_____ drives me crazy.

June 12
What's an Aye Aye?

———————————

June 13
Worst Vacation Ever

———————————

June 14
Easter has the bunny. Christmas has Santa. Who is the character for Flag Day?

June 15
Tomorrow is Father's Day. Make dad a card or present!

_____

June 16
What's an Unskerblugen?

_____

June 17
Best Vacation Ever

June 18
The rabbit's worst habit is…

_____

June 19
Best Pinata Ever

_____

June 20
Worst Pinata Ever

June 21
Time to simmer in the summer…

_____

June 22
There ain't no cure for the summer time blues…

_____

June 23
Fantastic Fred the Fabulous Frog

June 24
Travel in the Future

June 25
Obstacles are what we see when we take our eyes off the goal.

June 26
What's a Troglodyte?

June 27
Draw paradise.

_____

June 28
May the _____ be with you.

_____

June 29
Wisdom is proven right by its actions.

June 30
A spider was surfing the web…

_____

July 1
It's National Anti-Boredom Month. Make something exciting!

_____

July 2
If life is a highway, where does yours lead?

July 3
We hold these truths to be self-evident, that all men are created equal…

July 4
…and the rocket's red glare, the bombs bursting in air…
Happy Independence Day

July 5
We hold these truths to be self evident

July 6
The obligation of every human being is to...

_____

July 7
The first Sunday in July is Build a Scarecrow Day. You know what to do.

_____

July 8
There's gonna be fireworks, and not the good kind!

July 9
Firefly Fantasia

_____

July 10
Best Thrill Ride Ever

_____

July 11
The old swimmin' hole...

July 12
The cruel words of one are worth nothing compared with the uplifting shouts of many. On which one do you focus?

_____

July 13
Worst House Pet Ever

_____

July 14
Best House Pet Ever

July 15
Ask any rabbit, rabbit's feet are not lucky!

_____

July 16
Worst Tourist Attraction Ever

_____

July 17
I was happier before they invented_____.

July 18
When did you first know you were an artist?

_____

July 19
Hammerhead, Mandrill and other animals named after tools

_____

July 20
Design a sign for your dream business.

July 21
Welcome to my nightmare…

_____

July 22
Draw your favorite vacation memory.

_____

July 23
Draw the elephant in the room.

July 24
Worst bedtime story ever

_____

July 25
What's a disgronificator?

_____

July 26
Worst Road Sign Ever

July 27
Stop the madness, start the…

_____

July 28
Fairy God-monster

_____

July 29
Draw the strangest animal you've ever seen.

July 30
Draw your favorite musical instrument.

_____

July 31, 2013
My dream house...

_____

August 1
It's Admit You're Happy Month. What makes you happy?

August 2
Life is a journey, not a destination.

_____

August 3
Samurai Skunk

_____

August 4
The dog at my homework. What did the cat do?

August 5
Worst camping trip ever

_____

August 6
It's Andy Warhol's birthday, do a self portrait in his style or sketch your favorite household product ala the Campbell's Soup can.

_____

August 7
Design a T-shirt for your home town.

August 8
Draw something that inspires you.

_____

August 9
A group of monkeys is called a troop, a group of frogs is called an army and a group of vultures is called a committee.

_____

August 10
The complexity of simplicity.

August 11

You don't get to choose what happens to you, but you do get to choose how you respond.

———————————

August 12

The Adventures of Cardboard the Box Turtle

———————————

August 13

Worst Sports Team Ever

August 14
Worst Sports Mascot Ever

August 15
On this date in 1969 the Woodstock festival began. Create a piece of art that would fit that period.

August 16
The best artist at Woodstock was…

August 17

Of course most of the Woodstock artists are pretty old now. If they did a reunion they might have to call it_____.

_____

August 18

One thing we all have in common is...

_____

August 19

It's Gene Roddenberry's birthday. Draw your favorite Star Trek character or something out of this world.

August 20
Highway Robbery

_____

August 21
I dream of a world where…

_____

August 22
The obligation of every artist is to...

August 23
Create a new reality show for the fall season.

_____

August 24
The highlight of my summer was…

_____

August 25
The ultimate sand castle...

August 26
The ultimate tree house...

_____

August 27
Draw yourself in your current job.

_____

August 28
Draw yourself in your dream job.

August 29
Create the route from your current job to your dream job.
(Then follow it.)

_____

August 30
Why does summer seem to go so fast?

_____

August 31
Sometimes you're the windshield, sometimes you're the
bug.

September 1
Draw your favorite childhood cartoon.

———————————————

September 2
It's National Self Improvement Month. What do you want to improve?

———————————————

September 3
Life is like a box of _____.

September 4

The thing I love (or dread) about back to school is_____.

_____

September 5

The best way to deal with a bully is_____.

_____

September 6

Cardboard Skyscraper

September 7

Success belongs to those too stubborn or stupid to realize they cannot succeed.

_____

September 8

A life without limits is…

_____

September 9

True beauty is found in…

September 10

The best way to overcome a problem is to be a part of the solution.

_____

September 11

It's been ___ years since the planes hit the towers. How will you remember?

_____

September 12

Who do you think you are?

September 13
Worst Homework Assignment Ever

_____

September 14
Better to be silent and thought a fool than to open your mouth and remove all doubt.

_____

September 15
If you want to know whether or not you're a leader, look over your shoulder and see if anyone is following you.

September 16
Draw a pop-art robot!

_____

September 17
The rat race is over. The rats won.

_____

September 18
What does it take to be a hero?

September 19
Amish computer

_____

September 20
No guts, no glory. No glory, no_____

_____

September 21
Do they call it fall because the weather goes downhill from here?

September 22
What does "peaceful" mean to you?

_____

September 23
Love is_____.

_____

September 24
It's Jim Henson's Birthday! Draw your favorite of his characters.

September 25

Give a man a fish and he'll eat for a day, teach a man to
_____ an he'll _____.

_____

September 26

Smile, it makes people wonder what you're up to.

_____

September 27

Use every crayon in the box.

September 28
If you don't like the state of your world, create a better one.

September 29
It may be 5:00 somewhere, but somewhere it's also 1:43.

September 30
The frog in the kettle...

October 1

One word, Oktoberfest!

_____

October 2

The colors of Autumn

_____

October 3

Time to winterize the _____.

October 4
Spooky Hay Ride

_____

October 5
Maise Maze

_____

October 6
Bobbing for_____

October 7
Harvest Moon

_____

October 8
Mouse Pad

_____

October 9
Worst Halloween Costume Ever

October 10
The strangest thing I ever found in my trick or treat bag was…

_____

October 11
My Halloween Costume (past, present or future)

_____

October 12
You shall not pass...

October 13

Worst Movie Monster Ever

_____

October 14

Best Monster Movie Ever

_____

October 15

Create a creature.

October 16
Create an alien.

_____

October 17
Loch Ness Monster vs. Bigfoot

_____

October 18
Vampires vs. Werewolves

October 19
I'm melting…

_____

October 20
It's all fun and games until the flying monkey show up.

_____

October 21
Draw Godzilla's next opponent.

October 22

Dragon wagon

———————————

October 23

Are you sure there's nothing hiding in the closet?

———————————

October 24

Draw the monster under your bed.

October 25

It's Picasso's Birthday, (and mine!) In his honor, do a self portrait in his style.

_____

October 26

The fourth Saturday in October is Make a Difference Day.

_____

October 27

What scares you?

October 28

Design a new Halloween decoration.

_____

October 29

Design a new movie monster.

_____

October 30

Best Halloween Costume ever

October 31
Trick or Treat, Smell My Feet, Give Me Something Good to Eat

_____

November 1
It's National Novel Writing Month. Design the cover for your novel.

_____

November 2
Snow White actually had nine dwarves. Tell us about the two no one wants to talk about.

November 3
Henri Matisse passed away on November 3, 1954. In his honor create a piece of art using nothing but cut paper.

_____

November 4
I was born to be_____.

_____

November 5
Draw a politician.

November 6

There's a new third political party. The Democrats have the donkey. The Republicans have the elephant. Name the third party and what is their mascot.

_____

November 7

Make an avant garde portrait.

_____

November 8

Time waits for _____.

November 9

Make a poster for an event in the style of a propaganda poster.

November 10

Reality is what we experience when we cease to be creative.

November 11

Today is Veteran's Day. Create something to thank a veteran.

November 12
An Elephant and a Donkey started fighting. Everyone lost.

———————————————

November 13
Worst Political Ad Ever

———————————————

November 14
It's Monet's birthday. Create a piece of art in the impressionist style.

November 15

You were born unique. Stay that way!

November 16

You were created to create.

November 17

Yesterday is gone. Tomorrow never comes. It's always today. Use today for all it's worth.

November 18

Create an abstract pattern.

November 19

Create a character with character.

November 20

Create a harvest themed still life.

November 21

If I was any happier, I'd be_____.

_____

November 22

Re-illustrate a page from a favorite children's book.

_____

November 23

Make a flip book.

November 24

Who can you use your talent to serve today?

_____

November 25

Baby New Year 2013 today (age progression).

_____

November 26

What your turkey is thinking right now. (Pretend he's not already in your freezer.)

November 27

Gratitude is an attitude.

_____

November 28

What are you thankful for?

_____

November 29

It's black Friday. If you're shopping , design your protective gear. If you're staying at home draw the crazy people who aren't.

November 30

It's the most wonderful time of the year… Why?

_____

December 1

If they didn't use a light bulb to represent and idea, what would they use?

_____

December 2

It's Georges Seurat's Birthday. Do a work of art in pointillism (a work entirely made up of dots).

December 3
Make a hand-made holiday gift for someone special.

_____

December 4
I'm dreaming of a _____ Christmas.

_____

December 5
It's Walt Disney's Birthday. Draw your favorite of his characters.

December 6

If Santa is so cool, why does he make all the little kids at the mall scream?

_____

December 7

A date which will live in infamy…

_____

December 8

Rudolph the Red Nosed Reindeer II: Rudolph's Revenge

December 9
Heat Miser vs. Snow Miser

_____

December 10
What's your favorite holiday movie/special?

_____

December 11
Draw something symbolic of your holiday tradition.

December 12
Draw your favorite childhood toy(s).

_____

December 13
Worst Inflatable Yard Decoration Ever

_____

December 14
What's a yuletide?

December 15

My favorite thing about the holidays is…

_____

December 16

What's your opinion of snow?

_____

December 17

Create a unique way to display your holiday cards.

December 18

An actual use for a fruitcake

_____

December 19

Worst Christmas Sweater Ever

_____

December 20

Design a Christmas tree ornament.

December 21
Is it winter already?

_____

December 22
Snargy, Santa's most obnoxious elf

_____

December 23
Before Santa got the flying reindeer he tried_____.

December 24
How much milk and cookies can one man eat?

_____

December 25
Best Gift Ever

_____

December 26
It's Boxing Day. What on earth does that mean?

December 27

Make a collage from gift wrap and holiday cards.

_____

December 28

It's Stan Lee's Birthday. Draw your favorite comic book character.

_____

December 29

Think of your most important New Year's resolution and make something that reminds you to keep it.

December 30
The New Year's resolution I wish I kept is...

_____

December 31
And the award winning moment of the year was…